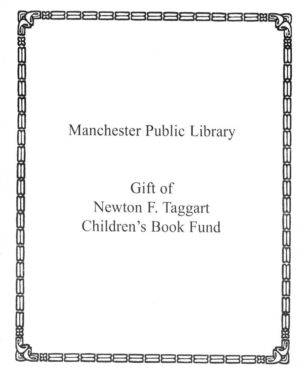

YOUR PERSONALIZED
INTERNET

NEWS UPDATE

The Best Airline, If You Have a Taste for Ad...

Adventurous travelers have a trick to finding a cheap fare: Book a ticket

The Airline picks your destination.

At least 50% of all revenue received by Company

International payments problems - 23 Mar

Over the following years I plan to focus more and more this side of the business and believe there is a huge potential to make a difference through design photography

Subscribe
for newspaper online

...g Global

...way for business.

LIVE updates   Photo   Exchange Rate   Currency Data   Global sources   Simple integration

News + Buzz

You can make international payments safety

Is this the fanciest way to eat bibimbap?

How c... getting rea...

World Stock

We are creating a sys... their own style and s...

Some young talented kid c... images and add cherry to i... takes a photo in New Yor...

We are creating a system where very talented cre... can develop their own s... share everything. Som... talented kid comes alo... can take better image... I'll open her images a... cherry to it to regain f... one spot. An amazin...

EXCHANGE RATE

Precent Change in the Last 24 Hours

Money Transfers
Advertisement

BY DUCHESS HARRIS, JD, PHD
WITH ELISABETH HERSCHBACH

Core Library

An Imprint of Abdo Publishing
abdopublishing.com

Cover image: The content we see on the Web is often shaped by what we seek out online.

abdopublishing.com

Published by Abdo Publishing, a division of ABDO, PO Box 398166, Minneapolis, Minnesota 55439. Copyright © 2018 by Abdo Consulting Group, Inc. International copyrights reserved in all countries. No part of this book may be reproduced in any form without written permission from the publisher. Core Library™ is a trademark and logo of Abdo Publishing.

Printed in the United States of America, North Mankato, Minnesota
102017
012018

Cover Photo: Shutterstock Images
Interior Photos: Shutterstock Images, 1, 8, 12–13, 22–23, 25, 38, 43; Jeramey Lende/Shutterstock Images, 4–5; Luca Pape/Shutterstock Images, 6; Krista Kennell/Shutterstock Images, 11; Eric Vega/iStockphoto, 15; Wave Break Media/Shutterstock Images, 16; J. Scott Applewhite/AP Images, 18–19; Red Line Editorial, 27; AP Images, 32–33; iStockphoto, 36–37

Editor: Patrick Donnelly
Imprint Designer: Maggie Villaume
Series Design Direction: Megan Anderson

Publisher's Cataloging-in-Publication Data

Names: Harris, Duchess, author. | Herschbach, Elisabeth, author.
Title: Your personalized internet / by Duchess Harris and Elisabeth Herschbach.
Description: Minneapolis, Minnesota : Abdo Publishing, 2018. | Series: News literacy | Includes online resources and index.
Identifiers: LCCN 2017947124 | ISBN 9781532113925 (lib.bdg.) | ISBN 9781532152801 (ebook)
Subjects: LCSH: Internet--Social aspects--Juvenile literature. | Information society--Juvenile literature. | Microcomputers--Juvenile literature. | Digital media--Social aspects--Juvenile literature.
Classification: DDC 302.231--dc23
LC record available at https://lccn.loc.gov/2017947124

CONTENTS

google

All   News   Videos   Images   More

About 11,190,000,000 results (1.45 seconds)

Google
https://www.**google**.com/ ▼
Search the world's information, including webpages, imag
features to help you find exactly what you're looking ...

Google Docs
More than letters and words. Google
Docs brings your ...

Google Maps ✓
Find local businesses, view maps and
get driving directions in ...

Google Photos ✓
All your photos are backed up safely,
organized and labeled ...

More results from google.com »

Top stories

CUSTOMIZING THE WEB

The Internet has put more information at our fingertips than ever before. With a few clicks, we can research any topic. Our searches return millions of results.

For Internet users, browsing the Web is easy. In fact, we usually take it for granted. But for the companies that run websites, sifting through all that data is a massive task.

DIGITAL OVERLOAD

As of June 2017, Google's search engine tracked approximately 130 trillion Web pages. That includes about 1 billion websites and

With Google and other popular search engines, information is easy to come by.

We use algorithms all the time when we do math.

more than 152 million blogs. An average of 6,000 tweets are posted on Twitter every second. Every minute, 300 hours of YouTube videos are uploaded. Every day, 4.75 billion posts are made on Facebook.

It's hard to picture the vast scale of such numbers. All the data on the Web would fill more than 305 billion pieces of paper. If you stored all the data on CDs, the stack would reach the moon. To process all this data, people use complex formulas called algorithms.

ALGORITHMS AND THE WEB

An algorithm is a set of step-by-step instructions for carrying out a task. When you follow a recipe or do your math homework, you are using algorithms. Surfing the Web, sending e-mail, downloading music—algorithms tell your computer how to complete all these tasks.

The algorithms that fuel the Web are automated processes. They are run by complex computer programs. Often we are not even aware that they exist. Yet algorithms have the power to shape what we see and do online. Consider the algorithms used by the popular social media site Facebook.

WHAT'S IN A NAME?

The word *algorithm* comes from Al-Khwārizmī. This Persian mathematician wrote a book about algorithms. Al-Khwārizmī lived around 800 to 847 CE. He was a scholar at the House of Wisdom in Baghdad, in what is now Iraq. This center of learning attracted thinkers from around the Muslim world. Al-Khwārizmī is best known for his contributions to algebra and the development of the Arabic numeral system. This system is still the most common way to represent numbers.

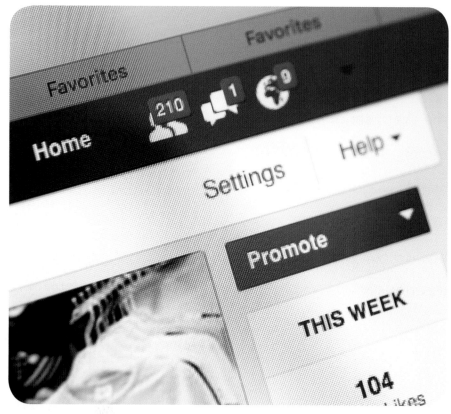

Facebook users with many friends may want to personalize their news feed.

FACEBOOK'S NEWS FEED

On average, Facebook users have more than 300 friends. Together these friends generate an average of 1,500 posts a day. This is an overwhelming amount of information. Few people could keep up with so many updates. Users would likely miss many of the most important ones.

Facebook's solution is to display posts selectively. When you log on to the site, you don't see everything your friends have posted. Instead, you see the posts that Facebook thinks you want to see. How does Facebook decide what to show you?

The company's algorithms track your patterns of behavior. This includes your clicks, shares, and "likes." This data is used to make predictions about your interests. These predictions then shape what shows up in your feed. Do you frequently react to sports news? Do you rarely click on posts about animals? Then your Facebook feed probably includes more football updates than cute kitten photos. Do you usually respond to your best friend but ignore your aunt? If so, you will see more of your best friend's posts than your aunt's.

THE FILTER EFFECT

Facebook's algorithms act as a filter. They control the information that you see. The result is a personalized feed. It is a collection of information customized for each user.

Personalized filtering is not unique to Facebook. Most social networking sites today use similar algorithms. Many other types of sites do as well. In fact, personalization is just about everywhere on the Web.

This new trend is changing the Web in important ways. The invisible algorithms shaping our online experience have wide-reaching effects. They affect the

Facebook executive Sheryl Sandberg spoke at the 2014 Fortune Most Powerful Women Summit.

privacy and security of our online actions. They also affect how we access news and other information. These changes are creating new challenges for the digital age.

CHAPTER
TWO

INFORMATION AT A PRICE

I n 2007, Yahoo vice president Tapan Bhat predicted "the future of the web is about personalization. It's about weaving the web together in a way that is smart and personalized for the user."

A decade later, his prediction rings true. Today, everything from shopping to news consumption is personalized online. Stores deliver personalized recommendations based on previous purchases. Customized ads follow us around from site to site. News sites allow us to determine the headlines we see.

Our past online shopping behavior contributes to the customized ads we see.

13

Even Google search results are personalized. Location, past browsing history, and our social networks can influence results. Let's say you search for "eagles." Which results show up at the top of the page? It may depend on whether you are a Philadelphia football fan or a wildlife enthusiast.

COSTS AND BENEFITS

For online companies, personalization means big business. Making online content more relevant to Web users means more clicks. More clicks translate into bigger profits.

Web users also find benefits to personalization. It helps us navigate the digital overload. We can easily find news, music, movies, and books that match our tastes. The ads we see are more likely to be for things we'd actually buy. What we see on social media is more likely to interest us. Our search results may be more useful.

Online newspapers, social media sites, and other websites are full of advertisements.

Yet there is a trade-off. Personalization makes it convenient to use the Web. But we end up with less control over our own personal information.

ONLINE TRACKING AND PERSONALIZATION

Every time you click on a site, the website collects information about what you are doing online. The site Dictionary.com, for example, installs more than 200 tracking cookies and beacons each time you look up a word. More than 95 percent of other websites also install tracking files.

A technician examines the network equipment in a server room.

Cookies are tiny text files stored on your device. They are used to store information such as user preferences and passwords. Beacons are invisible files embedded in a Web page. They track your online activity, including what you click on and how long you spend on a page.

These tracking devices do not harm your computer in any way. However, they enable companies to collect vast amounts of data. This online tracking makes Web personalization possible. Yet the results, critics argue, are not always harmless.

BIG DATA IS WATCHING

The very large sets of data collected through online tracking are known as "big data." Computer algorithms look for patterns in the data. Based on these patterns, companies construct detailed profiles of our habits, lifestyles, interests, and identities.

Congress voted to repeal FCC privacy regulations in April 2017.

Websites use this information to customize their content. Ad companies use it for marketing purposes. That's why ads for Caribbean cruises might start appearing if you've spent time researching Jamaica.

But big data can also fall into other hands. Personal data can be sold to credit card companies, banks, and insurance companies. This data can then be used to make important decisions about loans or insurance coverage. Personal data could end up in

a police database. It could be used by government agencies for surveillance purposes. Increasingly, it is also vulnerable to hackers. In 2016 hackers stole the personal information of 360 million MySpace users. In 2013 and 2014, more than 1.5 billion Yahoo accounts were hacked.

These risks raise serious concerns about privacy and security. The fact that online tracking mostly happens without our knowledge makes the problem worse.

Usually, we don't know what data is being collected or how it will be used. We don't even know how accurate the information is.

Data tracking affects more than just online privacy and security. Some experts worry that it also affects the flow of information online. Data tracking drives the push to personalize Web content. But too much personalization, critics warn, can have important personal and social consequences.

STRAIGHT TO THE
SOURCE

In a 2010 article in the *Wall Street Journal*, journalist Nicholas Carr warned of the trade-off between personalization and privacy:

> *The greatest danger posed by the continuing erosion of personal privacy is that it may lead us as a society to devalue the concept of privacy, to see it as outdated and unimportant. We may begin to see privacy merely as a barrier to efficient shopping and socializing. That would be a tragedy. . . . Privacy is not only essential to life and liberty; it's essential to the pursuit of happiness, in the broadest and deepest sense. We human beings are not just social creatures; we're also private creatures. What we don't share is as important as what we do share.*
>
> Source: Nicholas Carr. "The Dangers of Web Tracking: The Great Privacy Debate." *Wall Street Journal*. Wall Street Journal, August 6, 2010. Web. Accessed September 27, 2017.

Point of View

Why does Carr think privacy is so important? Do you think his fears about the erosion of privacy are reflected in today's culture? Why or why not? Be sure to explain your opinion in detail and include facts and details to support your own point of view.

CHAPTER THREE

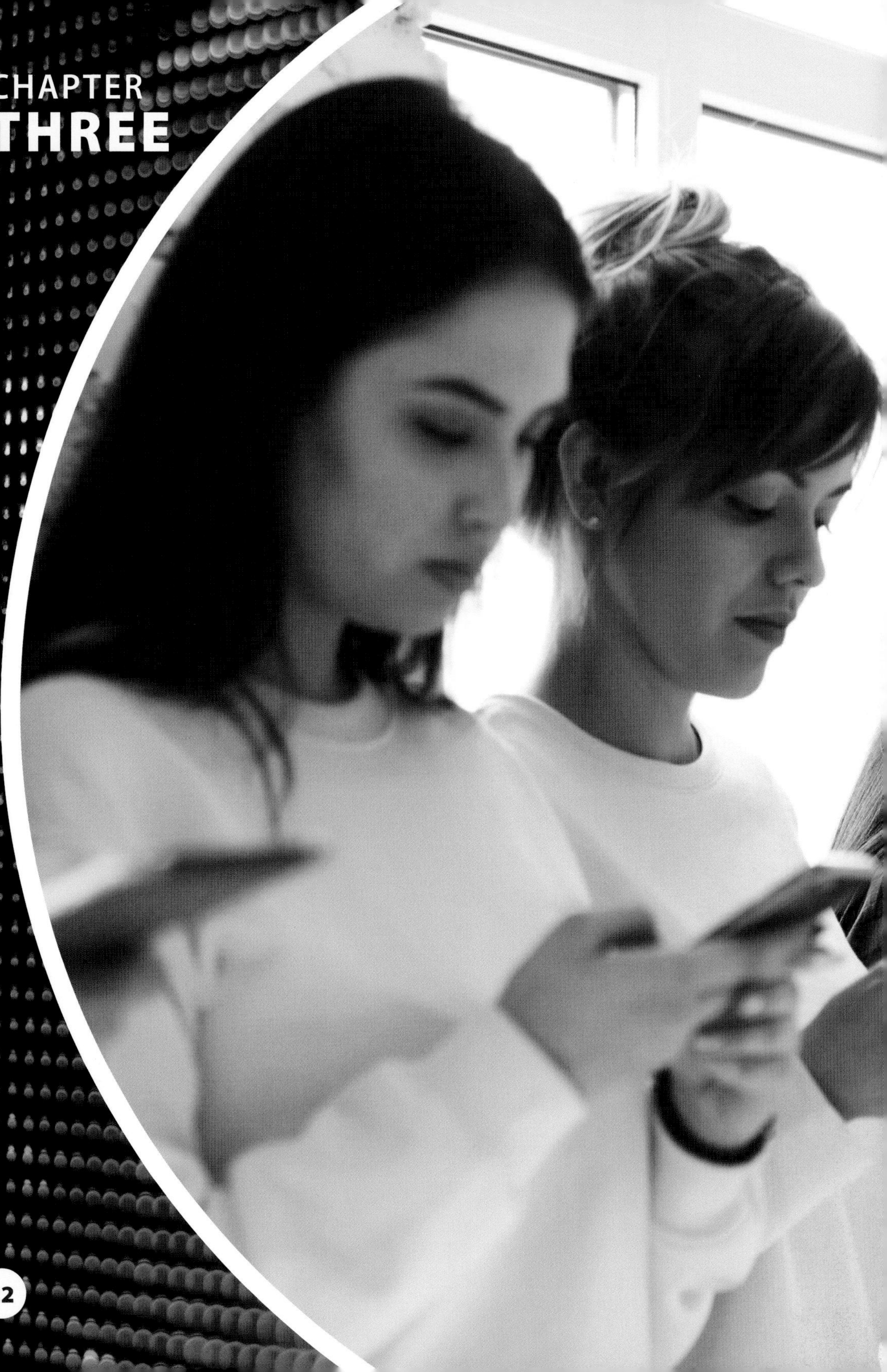

FILTER BUBBLES AND ECHO CHAMBERS

T he Internet is a wonderful resource. We can connect online with people from all over the world. We can discover a wealth of new ideas and information. It's best to be careful, however. A personalized Internet experience can make it too easy

Every Internet user has a different online experience, based on their personalized "filter bubbles."

to filter out information. Instead of discovering new interests and perspectives, we can end up narrowing our horizons. This creates what researchers call "filter bubbles."

BUBBLE TROUBLE

Filter bubbles arise because of the way personalization works. Algorithms analyze our online actions. Previous clicks, shares, and Web searches count as evidence of our interests. Those interests are used to select online content for us.

This means that our past online actions will shape the information we see in the future. Over time, the range of things we see may narrow. Topics we have liked in the past make it through the filter more easily. New information, such as opposing views on those topics, might get filtered out.

Filter bubbles can take a personal toll. They can limit our opportunities for personal growth. We can become trapped in our own biases without realizing it.

A healthy democracy depends on people listening to viewpoints other than their own.

But there are also social consequences.
Personalization is good at helping us find information
we want to hear. For citizens in a democracy, however, it
is just as important to be exposed to other perspectives.

SERENDIPITY

An old fairy tale tells the story of three princes from Serendip (modern-day Sri Lanka) in search of a missing camel. Along the way, they stumble on a series of lucky discoveries. This is where the word *serendipity* comes from. Serendipity means finding valuable things by accident. It plays a crucial role in scientific innovation and artistic creation. Random connections can lead to unexpected insight and learning. That can spark creative breakthroughs. Some critics argue that personalization algorithms are bad for creativity. This is because they are designed to filter out random ideas. As a result, they leave less room for serendipity.

WELCOME TO THE ECHO CHAMBER

Healthy public debate is essential for a healthy democracy. This requires people to be well informed. We also need to be exposed to views that challenge our own. And we need a baseline of shared facts.

If we get too much of our news and political commentary from personalized sites, healthy debate can be harder to achieve. The Web can become an

SOCIAL MEDIA AND THE NEWS

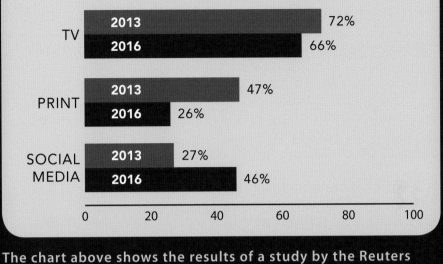

Percentage of Americans Getting Their News from TV, Print, and Social Media

TV
- 2013: 72%
- 2016: 66%

PRINT
- 2013: 47%
- 2016: 26%

SOCIAL MEDIA
- 2013: 27%
- 2016: 46%

The chart above shows the results of a study by the Reuters Institute for the Study of Journalism. What trends do you see in the data? Given what you read in this chapter, why do you think these trends might lead to more or less concern about the effects of echo chambers?

echo chamber where people hear voices that say what they already believe.

Echo chambers create different channels of information for different people. As a result, people can end up with very different visions of reality. This sharpens political divisions. In turn, it becomes harder to find common ground.

Echo chambers are especially a problem on social media sites. This is because people tend to have like-minded friends. As a result, the news and opinions our friends share will likely reinforce our own viewpoints. We are less likely to encounter information that challenges our beliefs. This can give us a skewed perception of issues. It can also make it easy for misinformation and fake news to spread. The 2016 US presidential election included many examples of this.

SOCIAL MEDIA ECHO CHAMBERS AND FAKE NEWS

In July 2016, a website reported that Pope Francis had endorsed Donald Trump for president. The story went viral on social media. It got more than 960,000 shares and comments on Facebook. By comparison, the top performing Facebook story from the *New York Times* got only about 370,000 shares and comments. The problem? Pope Francis never endorsed Trump. It was fake news.

Fake news like this spread like wildfire on social media throughout the presidential campaign. In many cases, fake stories got more social media attention than factual news stories. Some political analysts even think that fake news might have influenced the election results.

Why does fake news spread so easily? Experts think that it has to do with confirmation bias. People tend to believe information that confirms the views they already have. Social media echo chambers make this problem worse. People are shown only things they are likely to agree with.

The results can be dangerous. In December 2016, for example, a gunman opened fire in a pizzeria in Washington, DC. He had read online that the restaurant was harming children with the help of Democratic nominee Hillary Clinton. This was a debunked conspiracy theory. It had gone viral on social media at the end of the 2016 campaign.

FURTHER EVIDENCE

Chapter Three discusses how filter bubbles can lead to biased information. What are some of the main points of this chapter? The term *filter bubble* was first coined by Eli Pariser. Watch his TED Talk below or read the accompanying transcript. Find a quote that supports or expands on the chapter's main points.

BEWARE ONLINE "FILTER BUBBLES"
abdocorelibrary.com/your-personalized-internet

STRAIGHT TO THE
SOURCE

John Stuart Mill was a British philosopher and economist in the 1800s. In this passage he explains the importance of being exposed to different points of view:

It is hardly possible to overrate the value, in the present low state of human improvement, of placing human beings in contact with persons dissimilar to themselves, and with modes of thought and action unlike those with which they are familiar. . . . Such communication has always been, and is peculiarly in the present age, one of the primary sources of progress. To human beings, who, as hitherto educated, can scarcely cultivate even a good quality without running it into a fault, it is indispensable to be perpetually comparing their own notions and customs with the experience and example of persons in different circumstances from themselves.

Source: John Stuart Mill. *Principles of Political Economy with Some of Their Applications to Social Philosophy.* Boston, MA: C. C. Little & J. Brown, 1848. Print. 174.

Back It Up

Why does Mill think exposure to diversity is so important? Read back through Chapter Three. Find two or three points that support Mill's view. Write a paragraph defending Mill's view and explaining the evidence that backs it up.

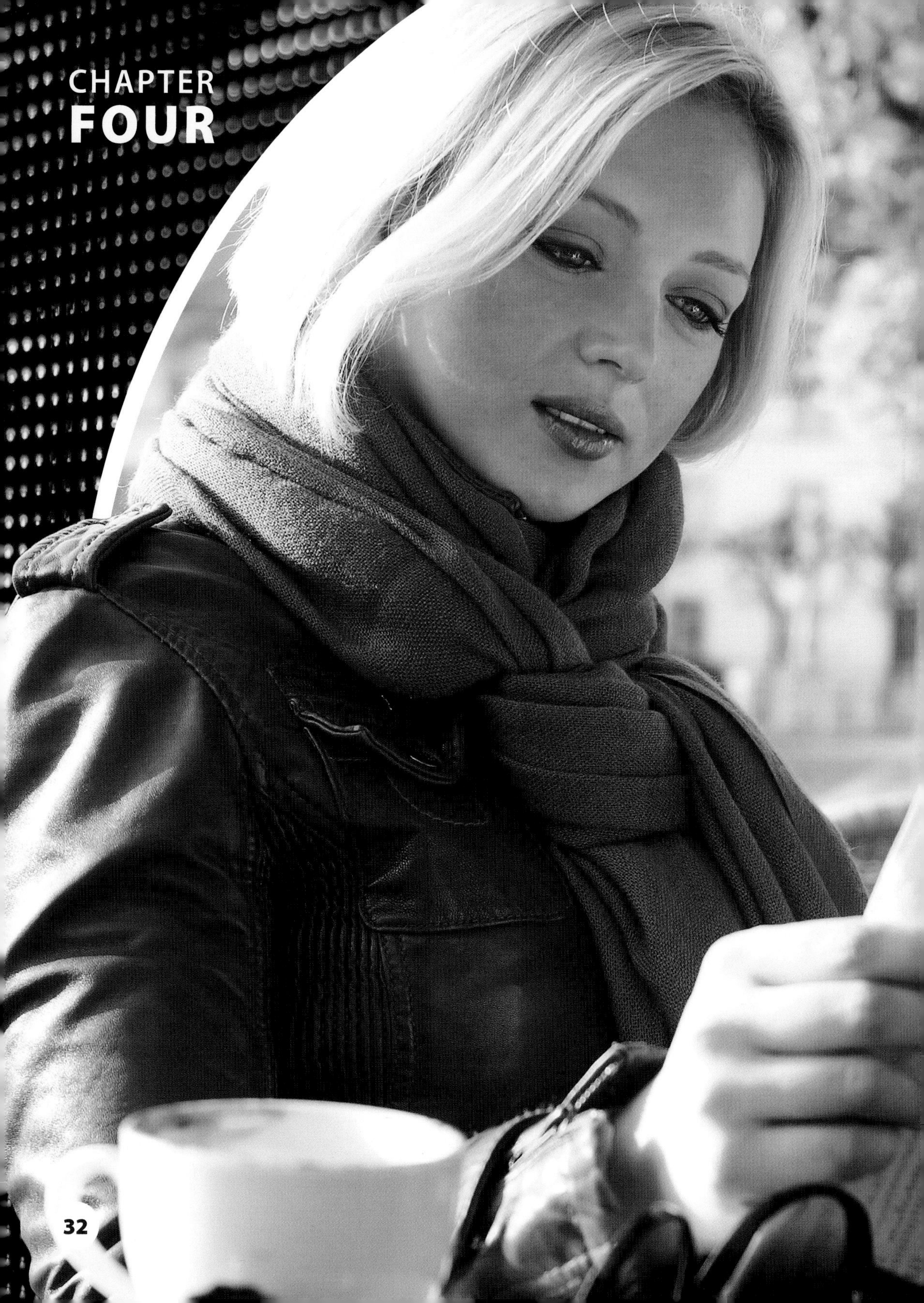

CHAPTER FOUR

BURSTING THE FILTER BUBBLE

Echo chambers are not unique to the Internet. Off-line, too, we often filter out opposing views and topics that do not interest us. We read magazines and books that reflect our interests and biases. We watch news channels and read newspapers that fit our preferred worldview. To some degree, filtering always happens. Nobody can pay attention to everything. Being selective about the news and information we consume is unavoidable.

HIDDEN BIAS

Internet filters, however, present unique challenges. This is because the algorithms used

Even off-line, people are selective about choosing what news they want to consume.

BUILDING BETTER ALGORITHMS

Social media sites constantly adjust their algorithms. Companies such as Facebook have tried to weed out fake news. Law professor and political scientist Cass Sunstein has some suggestions for building better algorithms. He argues that Facebook could use algorithms to identify when a user's feed is too skewed toward one viewpoint. Then users could click a button and see opposing views. Similarly, Facebook could provide a "serendipity button." This would allow users to see randomly selected material. These ideas could be tweaked for search engine results too.

to filter information on the Web are mostly invisible to us. For example, Google doesn't reveal the exact formula it uses to determine search results. Facebook's powerful algorithms are also secret. We don't know how information is filtered. Often we are not even aware that there is filtering going on in the first place.

Because we don't see what gets filtered out, we don't know what we're missing. This makes it difficult to evaluate bias. It makes it hard to tell how selective the information we're getting may be.

KNOWLEDGE IS POWER

Fortunately, you can take steps to minimize the effects of the filter bubble and to protect the privacy of your personal information. An important first step is to learn more about the sites you visit most often. Find out whether your favorite websites filter content. Carefully read the privacy policies of the sites you use. What information do they collect? What do they do with it? What privacy and security settings do they have?

Awareness puts us in a better position to evaluate how online tracking and personalization shape what we see. When possible, choose sites that are more transparent about how they filter content and use personal information.

CHANGE YOUR HABITS

Web users can't do much to change the algorithms that control the Web. But we do have control over our own

Internet habits. When our online patterns are varied, it is harder for computer algorithms to narrowly restrict what we see.

Make a habit of visiting many different types of websites. Read about a broad range of topics. Seek out

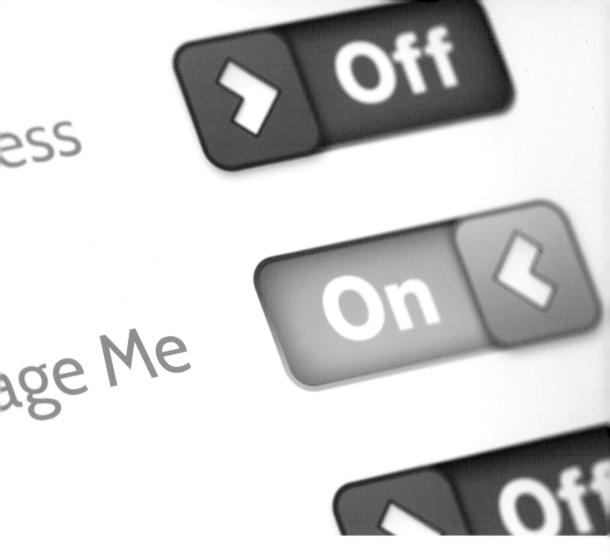

multiple perspectives on issues. Find new interests and explore new ideas. Finally, be sure to approach all the information you see online with a critical eye. Learn how to evaluate information. Learn how to recognize whether sources are reliable.

PROTECTING
PRIVACY

According to a Pew Research Center study, 93 percent of adults in the United States think it's important to control who can access their personal information. But a majority of Americans are not confident that online service providers will keep their data private and secure. The graphic below shows the percentage of Americans who have taken specific steps to protect the privacy and security of their online data. Which methods do you think are most effective? Why? What recommendations would you give to Web users who are concerned about online privacy?

Clearing History: 59%

Avoiding Using Real Name: 23%

Encrypting Data: 10%

Disabling Cookies: 34%

Using a VPN: 9%

COVER YOUR TRACKS

Every action you take online leaves a digital footprint. Websites personalize their results by tracking these footprints. When you cover up your footprints, there is less data available for companies to track. The Web results you get will be less biased.

There are several ways you can reduce your digital footprint. You can regularly delete the cookies that your Web browser uses

GOING INCOGNITO

The "do not track" setting of your Web browser tells companies not to track you. The privacy mode of your browser prevents it from storing data about the sites you visit. However, these built-in tools are not very effective. Many companies do not honor "do not track" requests. And using the privacy mode does not prevent your Internet protocol (IP) address from being tracked. A more effective alternative is to set up a virtual private network (VPN). This encrypts your data and hides your computer's IP address. The disadvantage is that reliable VPN services cost money.

Deleting certain types of files from your computer can help protect your privacy.

to identify you. You can also clear your browser's cache. This will erase the stored data that algorithms use to profile you. You can also permanently disable cookies. But if you do this, some sites may not load properly.

To ensure that your data is not stored in the first place, you can use anti-tracking tools. Some types of software detect and block tracking files. DuckDuckGo is an alternative search engine that doesn't track users. Unlike Google, it does not collect or share personal data. It also doesn't personalize results.

These tools can help you protect the privacy of your personal information. They can also help you break out of the bubble of the personalized Web.

EXPLORE ONLINE

Chapter Four mentions some ways to reduce online tracking. Read the article at the website below. Why did the author decide to stop using Google? What were some of the challenges she faced? Why did she think the benefits outweighed the challenges? Do you agree?

PRIVACY TOOLS: HOW I QUIT GOOGLE
abdocorelibrary.com/your-personalized-internet

FAST FACTS

- An increasing number of websites use algorithms to personalize online content. Personalized sites are designed to feed us information we'll find personally relevant—information that matches our interests and preferences.

- Websites personalize their content by tracking our online behavior: the links and pages we click on, the search terms we use, and our social media habits.

- Companies collect data about our online habits and create detailed profiles that are used to produce targeted ads and customized Web content.

- Companies tracking and collecting our personal data raises concerns about our online privacy and security.

- Tracking and personalization can also create online filter bubbles and echo chambers where we may get biased information.

- Developing good Internet habits and information literacy skills will help to minimize the effects of the filter bubble.

- Delete cookies and clear browser histories to reduce the amount of data companies can collect.

- Using search engines and software extensions that block trackers will also help us to be anonymous on the Web.

STOP AND
THINK

Tell the Tale

Try an experiment with a friend. Working on different computers, search for a word or set of words on Google. Compare the search results you and your friend get. Do you see any differences? If so, what do you think explains the differences? If not, why do you think this is the case? Write a paragraph comparing and contrasting the two sets of search results.

Surprise Me

Chapter Two discusses the privacy implications of personalization on the Web. What two or three facts about the topic did you find most surprising? In a few sentences, explain why you found those facts surprising.

Dig Deeper

Computer algorithms and big data are used for many purposes, not just for creating targeted ads or personalized Web content. With an adult's help, research some other ways that computer algorithms and big data are used today.

GLOSSARY

algorithm
step-by-step instructions for completing a task or solving a problem

beacon
an object embedded invisibly on a Web page or e-mail that collects information about your activity on a Web page or across multiple Web pages

confirmation bias
a tendency to believe information when it seems to confirm your existing worldview

cookies
small files installed on your device that store data about the websites you visit

debunked
shown to be false or unfounded

encrypt
to encode data so that only authorized users can understand it

incognito
having your identity concealed

polarization
division into different groups with sharply contrasting views

serendipity
the random occurrence of fortunate events by chance

ONLINE RESOURCES

To learn more about best practices for using the Internet, visit our free resource websites below.

Core Library
CONNECTION
FREE! COMMON CORE MULTIMEDIA RESOURCES

Visit **abdocorelibrary.com** for free Common Core resources for teachers and students, including vetted activities, multimedia, and booklinks, for deeper subject comprehension.

Booklinks
NONFICTION NETWORK
FREE! ONLINE NONFICTION RESOURCES

Visit **abdobooklinks.com** for free additional online weblinks for further learning. These links are routinely monitored and updated to provide the most current information available.

LEARN MORE

Eboch, M. M. *Big Data and Privacy Rights*. Minneapolis, MN: Abdo Publishing, 2017.

Freedman, Jeri. *When Companies Spy on You: Corporate Data Mining and Big Business*. New York: Cavendish Square Publishing, 2017.

ABOUT THE
AUTHORS

Duchess Harris, JD, PhD

Professor Harris is the chair of the American Studies Department at Macalester College. The author and coauthor of four books (*Hidden Human Computers: The Black Women of NASA* and *Black Lives Matter* with Sue Bradford Edwards, *Racially Writing the Republic: Racists, Race Rebels, and Transformations of American Identity* with Bruce Baum, and *Black Feminist Politics from Kennedy to Clinton/Obama*), she has been an associate editor for *Litigation News*, the American Bar Association Section's quarterly flagship publication, and was the first editor-in-chief of *Law Raza Journal*, an interactive online race and the law journal for William Mitchell College of Law.

She has earned a PhD in American Studies from the University of Minnesota and a Juris Doctorate from William Mitchell College of Law.

Elisabeth Herschbach

Elisabeth Herschbach is an editor, writer, and translator from Washington, DC.

INDEX